The Little Book for Busy Mums

How to Organize Your Life and Spend More Quality Time on You and Your Kids

Rachael Shephard

THE LITTLE BOOK FOR BUSY MUMS

Copyright © Octopus Publishing Group Limited, 2025

All rights reserved.

No part of this book may be reproduced by any means, nor transmitted, nor translated into a machine language, without the written permission of the publishers.

Rachael Shephard has asserted their right to be identified as the author of this work in accordance with sections 77 and 78 of the Copyright, Designs and Patents Act 1988.

Condition of Sale
This book is sold subject to the condition that it shall not, by way of trade or otherwise, be lent, resold, hired out or otherwise circulated in any form of binding or cover other than that in which it is published and without a similar condition including this condition being imposed on the subsequent purchaser.

An Hachette UK Company
www.hachette.co.uk

Vie Books, an imprint of Summersdale Publishers
Part of Octopus Publishing Group Limited
Carmelite House
50 Victoria Embankment
LONDON
EC4Y 0DZ
UK

www.summersdale.com

This FSC® label means that materials and other controlled sources used for the product have been responsibly sourced

The authorized representative in the EEA is Hachette Ireland, 8 Castlecourt Centre, Dublin 15, D15 XTP3, Ireland (email: info@hbgi.ie)

Printed and bound in Poland

ISBN: 978-1-83799-602-5
eISBN: 978-1-83799-603-2

Substantial discounts on bulk quantities of Summersdale books are available to corporations, professional associations and other organizations. For details contact general enquiries: telephone: +44 (0) 1243 771107 or email: enquiries@summersdale.com.

Neither the author nor the publisher can be held responsible for any injury, loss or claim – be it health, financial or otherwise – arising out of the use, or misuse, of the suggestions made herein.

Contents

Introduction 4

Mum Hacks 6

    Cleaning 7

    Organizing 31

    Lunchboxes and Mealtimes 55

Easy Self-Care Wins 78

Making Memories 108

Farewell 140

Introduction

"I've got too much time on my hands." Said no mum. Ever!

For the majority of mums, time is an elusive commodity, often stretched thin between balancing the demands of work, childcare, household responsibilities and personal needs. This constant juggling act leaves little room for rest, self-care or pursuing personal interests, making time management a crucial yet challenging aspect of daily life.

Historically, women have been expected to shoulder the lion's share of parenting, and even now, the heavy weight of a "mother's load" is often taken for granted. Gender roles have undoubtedly evolved toward greater equality in recent times, yet a significant disparity remains and societal expectations regarding the responsibilities and "unpaid work" of mums still have a long way to go. We are often expected to clean, organize the home, pay the bills, make school lunches (and let's not forget all that "help" with the children's homework!), coordinate mealtimes and make memories for our kids – and for those of you who have a career, there are additional factors to consider. Is it any wonder that mums get no time for self-care (or even time to eat on some days)?

This book is here to help you manage the disproportionate number of tasks expected of you, by offering a selection of time-saving hacks and tips on how to minimize stress and delegate without worry. It also contains a plethora of ideas for low-cost and no-spend activities you can enjoy and, most importantly, self-care suggestions. Whether you're looking for ways to streamline household tasks, balance work and family life more effectively or carve out precious moments for yourself, these strategies are designed to help you reclaim your time and energy. By incorporating them into your life, you can better prioritize your needs and enjoy your newfound free time – as well you should!

So, first tip. Remember that being a mum is a big part of your life, but the sum total of who you are is so much more than that.

Mum Hacks

Cleaning

"Oh, no," you cry, "not cleaning!" But the truth is that we often find ourselves juggling a multitude of housework tasks like it's some sort of Olympic sport – because let's face it, it is. This chapter is packed with genius hacks that will make you wonder why you ever considered hiring a cleaner or bribing your kids with money (okay, we may recommend a little bribery), just so they clean their rooms. From turning laundry into a game that would rival Mary Poppins's antics, to transforming your kitchen into a sparkly masterpiece (or at least, close enough), we've got you covered. And the best part? These tips are so simple, you'll have time to actually drink your coffee *before* it gets cold. So, grab your rubber gloves, your trusty vacuum cleaner and your ever-growing pile of laundry and let's turn your home into a zen-like paradise where you can finally relax in peace – well, almost.

PLANNING IS EVERYTHING

Creating a cleaning plan sounds like something only crazy-organized people do, but don't worry – we won't tell anyone! Writing down a cleaning strategy will save you time in the long run, and it's not exactly rocket science, so you can sit down and watch your favourite TV show at the same time.

Step 1: **Admit it's time**: First, acknowledge that your house didn't just "suddenly" become messy. It's been building up, and now it's time to take control.

Step 2: **Divide and conquer**: Start by dividing your house into zones. The kitchen, bathroom, living room, etc. It's a sneaky way to trick your brain into focusing on small chunks rather than the whole disaster. Plus, "Zone 1" sounds like you're planning something top-secret and important.

Step 3: **Schedule it like you mean it**: Pick a day and time for each zone. Monday for the kitchen, Tuesday for the bathroom and Wednesday for questioning your life choices. Be realistic. If you're not a morning person, don't schedule deep cleaning at 7 a.m. (No one needs that kind of negativity in their life.)

Step 4: **Spread it out**: You don't need to change your bedsheets more than once a week or deep clean the oven more than once every few months (or six), so space out your tasks accordingly. Areas that have the most footfall need regular attention, so keep these as your weekly tasks and leave a decent gap in the calendar for any deep cleaning. (There's an example cleaning schedule on page 10.)

Step 5: **Involve the minions**: Gather up your kids and get them involved. Assign them tasks based on their ability to clean (see page 14 for more info). You can even use a colour-coded weekly planner to make it easier for kids to follow.

Step 6: **Celebrate**: Once you've tackled your cleaning plan, reward yourself. Sit back, relax and put your feet up – before you antagonize your family by showing them their new responsibilities.

CLEANING TIME

Daily Tasks	Weekly	Every 6 Months
• Clean dishes • Wipe worktops • Tidy up toys	• Sinks and toilets • Vacuum carpets • Mop floors (or every fortnight) • Change bed linen • Dusting (or every fortnight) • Empty the tumble-dryer vent	• Deep-clean the oven • High level dusting (on tops of wardrobes, door frames, etc.) • Clear out the fridge and wipe clean • Clear out the freezer and wipe clean (defrost if required) • Clean windows
Every Few Days	**Monthly**	**Annually**
• Clear surfaces/put toys away/return items to drawers and cupboards • Empty out the bins • Laundry • Ironing (if you really have to!)	• Clean the microwave • Add rinse aid and salt to the dishwasher • Clean and vacuum the car • Wipe oven and clean inside the door • Descale the kettle	• Remove food from the kitchen cupboards/drawers and wipe clean • Dust light fittings and ceiling fans • Clean curtains

WHO NEEDS ELBOW GREASE?

Cleaning the kitchen can involve some serious elbow grease. Use these tips to negate the hard graft and save your energy for dealing with tantrums!

- **Microwave steam clean**: Heat a bowl of water and lemon juice in the microwave. It'll steam up, and all that hardened baked-bean sauce will just wipe away like magic. After that, make sure to use a microwave-safe cover (or plate) to prevent food splatters.
- **Easy oven cleaning**: Place a heatproof bowl filled with water and vinegar in the oven, heat it and let the steam loosen the grime. You'll find it wipes down easily while the oven is still warm – no elbow grease required.
- **Oven racks**: Oven and grill pan racks are notoriously difficult to get clean, but you can make it so much easier by soaking them in the bath with hot water and one cap of laundry detergent.
- **Non-stick cooking spray**: Lightly coat pans and baking dishes with non-stick spray to prevent food from sticking and reduce the need for scrubbing.

DELEGATE, DELEGATE, DELEGATE

Delegating house chores to children is like running a tiny household kingdom. You're the queen, and they're your loyal (but sometimes rather rebellious) subjects. The trick is to make them believe that chores are less like work and more like play.

- **Start with titles**: Kids love an important accolade. Don't just tell them to clean their room. Instead, say, "Congratulations! You've been promoted to Chief Toy Organizer!" Boom. Now they have a career (albeit in a voluntary capacity). Let them wear a pretend badge for extra motivation.

- **The art of negotiation**: Children are ~~unreasonable~~ expert negotiators. Offer choices like, "Would you prefer to vacuum or dust?" This way, they feel in control while still doing your dirty work (quite literally). It's all about creating the illusion of power while maintaining tight control over your mini army.

- **Turn chores into games**: Time how fast they can sort laundry or unload the dishwasher without breaking anything. You can even add levels: "You've completed Level One of Laundry Sorting; now can you handle Level Two – Folding

Towels?" Watch as they transform into tiny superheroes, determined to win at the cleaning game.

- **The strategic bribery plan**: Offer rewards like extra screen time, a treat or even just the satisfaction of having the tidiest bedroom in the house. Let's not kid ourselves – bribery works – so make it work for you.
- **Inspire future entrepreneurs**: If you want to offer money, suddenly you'll find they're not just cleaning – they're "investing" in their future, one chore at a time. Remember, you don't want to break the bank, so maybe only compensate for the bigger chores. Also price-cap each task and agree to contract terms before they start.
- **Lead by example**: Occasionally, you'll need to get in there and demonstrate how to clean properly. You can even exaggerate your excitement while spritzing to show them how *fun* it can be. Stick on your favourite tunes, crank up the volume and show them how it's done the *mum way*. They'll be joining you in no time.

AGE-APPROPRIATE CHORES

Every child is different, and you know yours best, but here is a rough guide to the ages when they might be ready to help with different chores.

Ages 2–3	Ages 7–10
• Dusting (they really love this one!) • Putting clothes in the washing machine and on the line/clothes airer • Picking up toys and putting them away	• Vacuuming • Helping to clean the car • Watering plants • Taking out the bins • Basic food preparation, like washing vegetables • Feeding pets
Ages 4–6	**Ages 11+**
• Setting and clearing the table • Making their own bed • Bundling socks into pairs • Folding laundry • Putting away the food shop (with a little help) • Tidying up their own room	• More advanced food prep – easy cutting tasks/basic knife skills • Washing dishes/unloading the dishwasher • Mopping floors • Mowing the lawn (with supervision) • Making their own packed lunch • Supervising younger siblings

CAR TROUBLE?

Cleaning your car doesn't have to feel like a full-day event. First, always keep a carrier bag in the car. When things start to get out of hand, simply grab the bag and toss everything in like you're conducting a clean-up on aisle *everywhere*.

For all those sticky, gross areas that your kids have painted with chocolate and yoghurt, wet wipes will do the trick quickly and easily. Pet hair taking over your seats? Grab a pair of rubber gloves, run your hand over the upholstery and watch as all the hair clumps together like magic. Use a handheld vacuum cleaner to finish.

And of course, never underestimate the power of a drive-thru car wash. Okay, so it only cleans the outside, but that's 50 per cent of the job done without breaking a sweat and it's far cheaper than a valet. Done is better than perfect, right?

SPILLS, STAINS AND OTHER MESSY MOMENTS

Kids are forever causing spills, stains and destruction. These tips are super handy for dealing with everyday inevitable mess and, with any luck, for bringing your mind back to a place of calm.

- **Glitter clean-up tool**: A creative and easy way to clean up glitter spills is by using playdough, which naturally picks up the tiny specks.
- **Give crayon-covered walls a blow-dry**: A hairdryer will soften crayon wax, making it easy to wipe off without too much effort.
- **Loosen and lift stains**: Blot and dab stains on carpets and mattresses with pure vodka or soda water and let the area air dry.
- **Use bread for picking up broken glass**: A piece of bread is perfect for grabbing small, hard-to-see shards of glass after you've swept up the larger pieces.
- **Put the dishwasher on**: It's a fast way to sterilize dishwasher-safe baby toys (just make sure they aren't cleaned together with dirty dishes!).

THE ART OF SKIM-CLEANING

Keeping your home looking presentable doesn't have to mean hours of hard work, thanks to the art of skim cleaning. This quick, efficient approach is perfect for maintaining a tidy space without the effort of a deep clean. Skim cleaning focuses on the high-traffic areas and visible surfaces, giving the illusion of a spotless home.

For bathrooms and kitchens, simply wipe down surfaces to remove marks and smudges, and give taps a quick shine with window cleaner. Run the vacuum cleaner over the main living spaces and use a bit of polish to dust key areas like coffee tables or shelves. You don't need to tackle every nook and cranny – just the spots that catch the eye. Rather than scrubbing your home from top to bottom, you'll achieve a clean and fresh atmosphere with minimal effort. (Save the deep cleaning for when you have more time or need to reset your space.)

WHEN I'M CLEANING WINDOWS

Cleaning windows with vinegar and newspaper sounds like something your grandmother swore by, and guess what? She was onto something!

Grab a spray bottle and mix equal parts white vinegar and water. Spray the solution all over the window like you're tagging it with graffiti. Let it sit for a minute or two. Skip the fancy cloths, glove-up, grab an old newspaper and scrunch a few pages into a ball. Rub the window down in circular motions like you're buffing a car. Using newspaper helps give the glass a streak-free shine because, unlike cleaning cloths, it has no lint, but remember to change the newspaper regularly to avoid ink transferring. For patio doors, use the same method, but when you're done, spray with a homemade sticky paw-print repellent. Simply mix 1 tablespoon each of white vinegar, rinse aid and washing-up liquid with ½ cup warm water in a spray bottle. Alternatively, you can buy ready-made water repellent to spray on the doors after cleaning.

ESSENTIAL OILS

Using essential oils is an easy way to make your home smell super fresh. They have a multitude of uses and are cheaper than buying loads of different smellies.

Start by picking your favourite essential oil – lavender for relaxation, lemon for a zesty uplift or eucalyptus for a refreshing spa scent. Add a few drops to a diffuser and your home will smell like a fancy boutique. To create your own room spray, mix a few drops of essential oil with water in a spray bottle and give it a shake. Spritz around the room, and voilà! For a slow-release aroma, add a few drops of oil to some cotton balls and place them behind the radiators – the heat will help to disperse the scent. Essential oils are also a perfect floor cleaner. Simply add a few drops to a bucket of hot water mixed with a cup of white vinegar and mop away.

LET IT GO

Let's get real for a second: trying to maintain a house that looks like a show home is basically like trying to paint the Forth Bridge – beautiful idea, but it's not going to happen unless you've got an army of cleaners who *never* stop working. The only thing you really achieve is burnout. Here's why you should let go of dream home perfection and embrace the "lived-in" look.

First of all, we all know that the second you finish deep cleaning every inch of your house, a tornado of toys, laundry and crumbs will magically appear from nowhere. Why aim for a spotless house when, within minutes, someone's going to smear chocolate on the sofa or leave Lego landmines across the floor?

Mums already work hard enough, whether it's wrangling kids, running errands or managing a household. You deserve a break from scrubbing floors and fluffing pillows like you're staging an open-house day. Instead, embrace the skim clean: wipe down the kitchen counter, swish the toilet brush and give the vacuum cleaner a quick run through the main areas. Good enough? *Absolutely!*

You know what's more important than having a pristine home? Your sanity. Those extra hours spent removing every speck of dust could be better used for things like catching up on sleep or doing something you enjoy. Your home should be a place of comfort, not a museum exhibit.

So, let go of the show-home dream. Aim for "clean-ish" rather than magazine-cover perfection. Trust us, nobody's judging your dusty skirting boards, and if they are, hand them a cloth and tell them to do it. Your time is too precious for that nonsense.

LEMON TRICKS

There are many natural alternatives to chemical cleaning products. Lemon and bicarbonate of soda (baking soda) bring some serious zesty, chemical-free energy to your home. Here's how to work their magic.

- **Dirty sinks**: Sprinkle bicarbonate of soda like it's fairy dust, then cut a lemon in half, squeeze it and use it to scrub like you're polishing a genie lamp. Watch your sink shine and maybe, just maybe, a genie will grant you a clean house (no guarantees).

- **Bathroom grime**: Mix equal parts lemon juice and bicarbonate of soda into a bubbly volcano of cleanliness and bang! You've got yourself a homemade super scrub.

- **Stubborn stains**: Combine the two into a paste, slap it on the mess and leave for an hour. It's like giving stains a spa treatment: they'll disappear, and your house will thank you. Plus, it's chemical free. Perfect if you have little ones crawling around.

REDUCE THE MESS

All mums know that cleaning up after the rest of the family is a never-ending mission, especially at mealtimes. Here are some easy ways to at least reduce the cooking mess (and keep the will to live).

- **Line the oven**: Line the bottom of your oven with a removable liner. Cook dinner, remove the liner and voilà! No scrubbing involved as the liner can be easily wiped clean.

- **One-pot wonders**: Why use 10,000 pots when you can use one? The less you use, the less you wash. See pages 72–73 for some one-pot recipe ideas.

- **Keep microfibre cloths handy**: They are perfect for wiping up spills and messes before they stain the worktop – and save using 1,000 paper towels.

- **Blender rinse cheat**: After using your blender, don't scrub it. Just fill it with water, add a drop of washing-up liquid and blend again. It's basically a self-cleaning robot!

BATHROOM TACTICS

Let's face it – cleaning the bathroom is nobody's idea of fun. But with a few simple tricks, you can make this dreaded chore quicker and easier. Start by spraying the bath, shower and sink with an all-purpose cleaner or limescale remover if you live in a hard-water area. Let it sit for about 10–15 minutes to loosen grime and soap scum. While it's working its magic, tackle the toilet and floor. Use disposable cleaning wipes for a super-speedy clean.

Next, grab a squeegee for the shower screen, tiles and mirrors. After rinsing away the cleaner, a quick swipe with the squeegee eliminates streaks without needing extra effort or glass cleaner. For taps and other shiny surfaces, use a microfibre cloth with a spritz of water or mild cleaner to leave them sparkling.

By breaking the job into manageable steps, you'll save time and energy. Plus, staying on top of regular, small cleans will make deep-cleaning days far less daunting. Job done!

HELPFUL GADGETS

There is no harm at all in spending a little extra money to make your life easier. So, why not bring in some gadgetry to do the dirty work for you? Okay, spending money on cleaning gadgets might seem indulgent, but honestly, it's an investment in your sanity.

Robot vacuums? Absolutely. Let that little beast run around like a futuristic pet, sucking up crumbs and dust while you sit back and relax. Steam-mops? Yes, please! They're basically magic wands for your floors. No scrubbing required and they sterilize the floor as they go: perfect if you have little ones crawling around.

And think about it: if a gadget saves you time, that all adds up to extra hours for doing important things like taking a bubble bath or enjoying a guilt-free slab of cake.

So go ahead, splurge a little on those cleaning gadgets. You're not lazy – you're just embracing the twenty-first century!

THE LAUNDRY WAR

Laundry has a way of transforming into a full-blown Everest situation if you're not careful. One minute, it's just a few socks and school shirts, the next, you can't see over the top of the mountain of clothes. The secret to avoiding this? A little-and-often approach.

Tossing in a quick load every other day (or daily if you've got a big family) keeps things manageable and prevents that moment of terror when you realize everyone needs to start turning their underwear inside out.

To speed up this dreaded task, utilize the 15-minute wash cycle for all clothes that aren't soiled and just need a freshen up. Add a dry towel to the tumble dryer (if you have one) and your clothes will dry much faster too!

Finally, to protect your socks from being mysteriously sucked into the ether, you need a mesh bag that keeps them all together, preventing them from sneaking off into the underworld of hidden laundry. No more frantic searches for that missing sock while silently accusing the washing machine of eating them.

NO TUMBLE DRYER? FEAR NOT!

Navigating the colder months without a tumble dryer is basically a test of patience, but fear not. You can still dry clothes without waiting 40 working days. First, get strategic with radiators – hang clothes nearby, but not too close or you'll have crispy towels instead of cosy ones. If you really want to go pro, drape a bedsheet over the radiator and clothes airer to create your very own homemade heat pod. This has the added benefit of drying your hefty bedsheets at the same time.

Next, consider using a fan. Yes, it's cold, but aim that thing at your laundry and it'll work like a mini wind tunnel.

If you're feeling super desperate, hairdryers aren't just for hair. Blast your clothes from the inside out to retain as much heat as possible. Okay, it's not exactly elegant, but neither is wearing wet knickers.

VACUUM BLITZ

Dust seems to multiply no matter how often you clean, and getting out the polish and cloth can feel like a pain in the proverbial. Instead, try using your vacuum cleaner to tackle multiple jobs quickly. Vacuum cleaners aren't just for floors – use them to clean curtains, blinds, skirting boards, cupboards, mattresses, sofas and even ceilings and walls. A vacuum cleaner with attachments can get into tricky corners and suck up cobwebs, making cleaning much faster and easier. You can even use the vacuum to get rid of crumbs in the toaster, food cupboards and on fridge shelves. Just make sure you use the correct attachment for the job.

And to avoid that musty vacuuming smell, add a bit of bicarbonate of soda or a few dryer sheets to the main compartment or put a few drops of essential oil in the filter. It's the ultimate multitasking cleaning tool!

IF ALL ELSE FAILS

And there you have it, mum-cleaning 101. By now, you've hopefully mastered the art of balancing a mop, a child, your time and those stubborn stains that seem to pop up quicker than a bargain hunter on Black Friday. Remember, the secret to a clean house is... well, lowering your standards. Just kidding (sort of). A spotless home is great, but happy kids and time for yourself is more important.

If all else fails, there's always the age-old trick of dimming the lights and ignoring the mess altogether. Declare it a "lazy day", and take back some time for yourself. Your fellow mum friends will understand, and actually, when you can let the small things go, you'll give them the licence to do the same.

At the end of the day, perfection is overrated. If everyone's alive and the house hasn't burned down, you're winning. Now, go grab that well-deserved glass of wine or a mocktail. You've earned it!

Organizing

Welcome to the wild world of organizing. As a fellow mum, you've probably realized by now that "organized chaos" is somewhat of a myth. But fear not. This chapter is here to help you declutter, sort and minimize the madness – without needing to find an extra three days in the week.

From the avalanche of school projects (seriously, how many crafting tasks can one child get?) to the mountain of photos zapping your phone memory, we've got hacks to help you get it together. You'll learn the art of clearing paperwork piles, creating miracle morning routines that save your sanity and tidying toys away in a manner that will rival Marie Kondo on her good days. We'll even tackle the digital jungle, so you can manage your schedule and finally get on top of the ongoing game of email Tetris. Ready to get organized? Let's dive in – you've got this!

THE RAINBOW EFFECT

Let's talk clothing organization, or as we like to call it, "The Rainbow Effect". Imagine opening your wardrobe and, instead of the usual chaos, you're greeted by a glorious rainbow of perfectly arranged outfits. Suddenly, finding that turquoise top you love isn't a 20-minute scavenger hunt through a sea of black leggings and mismatched hangers. Organizing your clothes by colour isn't just about looking Pinterest-perfect (though, let's admit it, that's a perk) – it's about making your life easier. Need something blue? Boom, right there. Wondering where your favourite green dress went? Not buried under a pile of laundry anymore! Plus, it's a handy way to convince yourself that maybe – just maybe – you don't need that fifth grey jumper. And let's be honest, who doesn't love a wardrobe that doubles-up as a rainbow-inspired therapy session? Embrace the rainbow, and your mornings will thank you.

DESIGNATED SPOTS

How many times a week do you end up hunting for your phone or your kid's glasses? If it's happening too often, it might be time to create designated spots for important items. Instead of spending 10 minutes tearing the house apart looking for your car keys, keep them in a bowl on a bookshelf, so you'll always know where they are.

This works wonders for kids' possessions, too. Try placing a large basket by the front door where school bags and shoes can "live". Rather than the daily "Where's my school bag?" or "I can't find my shoes" panic, they can actually leave on time – shoes on, homework in hand.

No one in the history of time has ever enjoyed the "Mum, I've lost my lunchbox" treasure hunt at 7 a.m., so make it one less thing to worry about. Designated spots mean less chaos, fewer search parties and more time to hit the snooze button or simply leave the house without a meltdown!

DECLUTTER LIKE A PRO

Ready to declutter your home in a way that doesn't involve a soul-sucking weekend, surrounded by junk you didn't know you had? Let's get creative – and a little inventive. First off, grab a big laundry basket. Walk around your house and toss in anything you don't love, need or can't identify. Yes, even that weird little ceramic cat your aunt gave you (she'll never know). Now, hide that basket out of sight for a week. If you don't miss anything, it's time to donate or dump it.

There is no exact science to decluttering your home, but the key to success is getting ruthless. Over time, the stuff we accumulate seems to actively reproduce. Just when you think you're getting on top of it, boom, it's Christmas or a birthday – and more stuff moves in. In reality, most of the things that are rammed into drawers and wardrobes never again see the light of day.

Decluttering has a multitude of health benefits. Research published in the journal *Current Psychology* found a direct link between procrastination and clutter. They found that physical clutter causes stress and anxiety, and adversely affects the ability to focus and process basic information. Additionally, a St Lawrence University study found that hoarders tend to sleep terribly – and who needs that in their life? Living in an organized space can benefit our mental health and increase our ability to focus. Organizing requires our brains to make decisions, plan and overcome procrastination – the result of which is lower levels of cortisol (the stress hormone). And what mum doesn't want to feel less stressed?

Decluttering doesn't have to be painful. Make it fun, mix in some trickery and before you know it, you'll have a clutter-free home – and maybe fewer ceramic cats!

PAPER ADMIN? SHRED IT!

Paper admin piles up, goes missing when you need it and somehow multiplies (it must have the same disease as the laundry). The solution? Shred it. Seriously, stop holding onto that stack of mystery paperwork like it's some sort of treasure. Instead, take photos of important documents and store them in a digital folder where you can actually *find* them. There are only a few paper documents you need to keep, such as a marriage certificate (well, you might want to shred this too!) and for the few that you must hold onto, get yourself a small binder so they're all in one place. If you're unsure whether you need to keep the original document, check online before you destroy it.

With digital storage, everything's at your fingertips, neatly labelled and searchable. Plus, you'll free up valuable space in your home. So, grab your phone, snap those documents and let the shredder do the rest. Your future clutter-free self will thank you.

TOY MAYHEM

Do you often find yourself wishing you had Mary Poppins's bottomless canvas bag when it's time to tidy up your kids' toys? We can't promise this sort of sorcery, but there are many toy storage solutions on the market that look nice and help you hide the mess. Adding clear plastic containers, wicker baskets or shelving units and cube organizers to your bedrooms and living rooms maximizes space to dump those toys and provides easy access. And a shoe storage holder that fits neatly on the back of a door is great for hiding excess teddies that your kids won't let you get rid of.

When it comes to the actual tidying up, instead of fixing up your house on autopilot, get your minions involved by turning it into a game. Set a timer and challenge them to a "race" to see who can put the most toys away before the alarm goes off.

THE MORNING SCRAMBLE

The morning scramble. The bane of every mum's existence. From the moment we wake up, there's breakfast to be made, the bathroom human conveyor belt to manage, little people to dress and big people to cajole out the door. It's the most stressful time of day for many mums and can set a chaotic tone before you've even stepped outside. The good news is that there are a few ways you can make your morning routine run seamlessly (ish). Here are five top tips for managing the morning madness.

- **Start the night before**: Plan ahead and get your kids bathed and showered, school bags packed and outfits laid out and ready for the morning. A few minutes of extra organizing will save you a lot of time and stress the following day.

- **Give yourself more time**: We all love the snooze button, but it's really not your best friend. Getting up even 15 minutes earlier than your kids can give you enough time to eat breakfast and drink a coffee in peace.

- **Follow a routine**: Kids respond well to routines, so make every day as predictable as you can. This way, they know exactly what is coming and that there is a schedule to stick to.

- **Make a picture schedule**: Better still, get your kids to make their own schedule. Have them draw pictures of the morning's activities, along with a little clock face next to each one. Children are more likely to stick to a routine they've helped devise, so get them onboard.

- **Play some music**: Music is scientifically proven to boost our mood, so turn up the radio and set the tone for the day by playing some happy tunes. It's hard to feel stressed when you're belting out your favourite hits!

SCHOOL PROJECTS

Homemade school projects are all very sweet and sentimental – until you have a gazillion of them taking over your house. Every week it's a new creation: macaroni necklaces, glitter-covered rockets and finger paintings galore. Lovely, but where are we supposed to store it all?

Here's a guilt-free hack: keep each masterpiece for a month, admire it, take a photo, then bin the project. You can keep anything that's particularly special, but for the rest, get your kids involved with the clear-out and have them make a scrapbook using those photos – it's a fun way to preserve the memory without causing upset by just throwing them out (the projects, not the kids, *obviously*).

For paper artwork, why not utilize a single picture frame and stack them all together? Simply rotate through the pictures periodically so they all get a chance to be displayed. This is another task that can easily be delegated to your offspring.

CUPBOARD ART

Do the insides of your kitchen cupboards resemble a bomb site? We've got an easy solution – decant everything you can into labelled containers. Transferring your kitchen cupboard ingredients into clear glass food containers is like creating a work of art. Every item stands in uniformed perfection, like soldiers in the army of organization. You'll feel like a domestic goddess every time you open the cupboard and see your storage-jar skyline.

No need to worry about the spaghetti coming out of the packet (how does it always end up upside down?). Need flour? There it is – without digging behind six bags of mystery powder to find it. Plus, those pesky mice can't break into your fortress of glass and your food stays fresher for longer! No more stale cookies or rock-hard sugar bricks.

SCRAP THOSE TO-DO LISTS

Mums are notorious for having paper trails that could rival the Yellow Brick Road. But what if you could tame this list-making beast? Imagine writing one *final* list – your ultimate nemesis. It would include everything: not just today's chores and tomorrow's to-dos but even things years into the future, like the looming family reunion or remembering to renew your passport before it sneaks up on you (again). Once it's all written down, you can transfer it to a digital calendar. Voilà!

Time allocated, dates set, reminders in place – no more writing endless lists on scraps of paper, which inevitably get lost or eaten by the dog. You can even set your events to recur weekly, monthly or annually so you only have to do this once. Instead of chasing crumpled notes around the house, you'll have a sleek, organized system. Your phone dings and you remember you have two weeks to renew that insurance or buy that gift.

Having your life organized on a digital calendar will stop you from fretting about when you can fit all of your to-do list into your day, because every task has an allocated space in your diary and you can clearly see where you're under or over committed. And if you have an emergency, simply reallocate your tasks for another day.

There is the added bonus that you'll also be saving a small forest by going paper-free. No more list-on-top-of-list madness, no more trees sacrificed in the name of birthday reminders. Plus, you'll never miss a trick and everyone will think you're an organization master – even if we know it's only because your phone keeps nagging you.

Above all else, make sure you factor in one task per day as a mandatory repeat feature – time for yourself. Protect your time like it's a newborn baby. You absolutely deserve it.

PICTURE PERFECT

Organizing the 20,000 digital photos on your phone is like tackling a virtual hoarding situation. First things first – get them off your device before they completely swallow your storage and leave you begging for space. Start by uploading everything to cloud storage or an external hard drive – think of it as decluttering your phone.

Now, if you can be bothered, organize those photos into neat little folders: "Holidays", "Baby's Firsts", "Random Food Pics You'll Never Look At Again" or even just by year. You could easily just leave the photos in one big file if you don't have the time to do this (or the will). Once you've downloaded your pics, get yourself a digital photo frame with a slideshow feature. Now, instead of these photos gathering virtual dust, you'll actually see them. Plus, every time you walk past, you can admire your past adventures... and the 57 pictures you accidentally snapped of your home screen!

MONEY MATTERS

When you think about organizing, you might picture tidying the junk drawer or dealing with that leaning tower of laundry. But guess what? Your finances can be just as messy.

Organizing your money may not be as satisfying as colour-coding your bookshelf, but it's way more important. Budgeting and paying bills on time can save you from last-minute panic attacks. Setting up auto-pay is a great time-saver and will ensure you never miss a payment deadline again. Also, regularly check your direct debits and cancel any you no longer use – you might be surprised how much you can save.

There are loads of free budget planners online to make financial management much easier and help you track your spending. There are also countless podcasts (*Afford Anything* and *HerMoney* with Jean Chatzky are good ones for beginners) about how to better manage your money. Plus, if your finances are in order, you can reward yourself by buying that fancy storage solution for all your perfectly folded jumpers. It's a win–win!

EMPTY INBOX? YES, PLEASE!

After even a day away from your inbox, you can expect to return to an avalanche of unread emails that could probably bury a small village. If you want to achieve the holy grail of an empty inbox, it's time to get ruthless.

First, unsubscribe to any newsletters you no longer need – this takes time in the short-term, but you'll thank yourself when you don't have to keep deleting new ones. Next, have a mass delete session (you can usually delete all emails from one address in one click) while you're watching TV. Finally, use folders to corral emails into neat little categories – like "School", "Bills" and a special one called "Action", which is code for "I'll deal with this… eventually". This way, you'll always know which emails require actual human effort.

Soon, you'll be a digital decluttering pro! And with your inbox sorted, you can spend your time doing something less painful, like booking a holiday to escape all the emails for a while.

"REMEMBER" NOTES

We all know that the morning dash is the equivalent of herding cats with a laser pen. You know, when you're trying to cajole the kids out the door, but halfway to the car you realize you've left behind the essentials or maybe your smallest child. Here's a tip: slap a "don't forget" list – keys, phone, purse, laptop, lunchboxes, etc. – on the back of the front door. Use brightly coloured paper or a neon Post-it so you can't ignore it.

Little reminders go a long way when you're up against the clock, so give it a whirl.

LOW-KEY, NOT LOW-FUN

In a world where social media showcases lavish celebrations with elaborate decorations, themed parties and costly gifts, it's easy to feel pressured to go all-out for Christmases and birthdays. However, low-key celebrations can be just as meaningful – often even more so – and might align better with your family's preferences and budget. The truth is that children often cherish the personal touches and quality time over flashy displays.

Instead of hosting a grand birthday bash, consider a small family celebration at home. Let your child choose their favourite meal or dessert and have a movie night, board game marathon or garden treasure hunt. You can decorate with simple, homemade crafts – like paperchains, balloons or fairy lights – which can double-up as a fun bonding activity. A heartfelt, handwritten card and a thoughtful but modest gift can make the day special without breaking the bank.

For Christmas, shift the focus from material gifts to meaningful traditions. Bake and ice cookies together, watch festive movies or go for a drive to see the local Christmas light displays. Create a "Christmas Eve box" with cosy pyjamas, hot chocolate and a book or small toy to build excitement. Instead of spending hours and money on lavish décor, let your children help with simple DIY decorations, like paper snowflakes or salt dough ornaments.

It's important to remember that children value the feelings and memories associated with these celebrations far more than how Instagram-worthy they are. By focusing on connection and shared experiences, you're teaching them that love and joy don't come from extravagance. Plus, a more relaxed approach allows you to truly enjoy the moments together, rather than stressing about meeting unrealistic expectations. In the end, it's the laughter, warmth and togetherness that your children will remember most.

THE DREADED DRAWERS

Whether it's the one stuffed with random papers and dead batteries, the kitchen cutlery drawer or your child's sock drawer – they always seem to hide what you need most. The ultimate fix? Drawer dividers. These ingenious organizers turn clutter into calm, giving every item its place and making your life infinitely easier.

This nifty trick can be used in just about any drawer in the house. No more digging through a sea of black knickers to find that one lonely white pair hiding at the bottom like it's playing hide-and-seek. Separators to the rescue! Your undies get their own VIP sections, and finding what you need not only becomes a breeze but saves a chunk of time too. In the bathroom cupboards, who needs fancy organizers when a simple cutlery insert can perfectly house toothpaste tubes, toothbrushes, cotton buds, creams and more. Pure genius.

In short, drawer dividers are the unsung heroes of domestic life. You'll wonder how you ever lived without them.

SUPERMARKET AVOIDANCE TACTICS

Who enjoys supermarket shopping? Er, no one. So why not get online and save your time? No more dodging rogue trolleys or battling with a self-checkout machine that's convinced your bananas are contraband. When you run out of something – milk, bread or your emergency stash of chocolate – you can update your online basket instantly, instead of hoping you remember during your next frantic trip. Plus, you don't need to drag your kids along with you, only to end up spending the entire time being pestered for sweets and toys! Even better, online shopping lets you use the magical "last order" function. Need groceries in a hurry? Just reorder the same essentials with one click. No aisle-wandering or getting distracted by deals on things you don't need – like a giant inflatable flamingo. Stay in your pyjamas, shop from your sofa and let someone else deal with the checkout stress.

BUDDY UP

Buddying up with other school mums is like joining a secret club where everyone's mission is survival! School runs, playdates and last-minute emergencies become much easier when you have a partner in crime.

If you've ever wished you could teleport, just to avoid the daily rush, here's the next best thing: childcare sharing. By dividing up the school runs with another mum, you cut your duties in half. On your newfound free mornings you get to sit back and reclaim a precious 20 minutes of peace. It's like finding gold dust in your day.

For parents, playdates are where happiness goes to die. If the thought of entertaining a pack of sugar-fuelled kids gives you a headache, a buddy can make it bearable. By rotating playdates, you get some guilt-free time off while knowing your kids are busy having fun with their friends – and, importantly, not destroying your living room or putting chocolatey paw prints on your walls.

School holidays can be a nightmare to navigate when you only get a few weeks of annual leave, but the kids are off for three times the amount of time. Divvying up the holidays with your mum friends is a great way to share the load and reduce stress at the same time.

It's not all about logistics. Having a fellow mum in your corner means you can swap advice, vent about the latest school drama or even team up for bigger parenting projects like planning birthday parties. You'll also have someone who understands when you need a quick chat, an emergency babysitter or just a good giggle.

The real beauty of this system? You're clawing back some time for yourself. Whether it's using that extra hour to finally catch up on your favourite show, go for a walk or simply sit in glorious silence, buddying up helps you balance it all.

DISCIPLINE

Organizing your life as a mum is like achieving domestic nirvana – everything in its place, to-do lists checked off and fewer frantic moments. But here's the secret: the real magic isn't just in the organizing, it's in the *discipline* to keep it up. Yes, discipline sounds as fun as watching paint dry, but it's the golden key that makes it all work. Once you've implemented a new schedule, reward yourself with a treat at the end of each month if you stick to it. Incentives aren't just for kids!

By being disciplined about the boring stuff – like sticking to that morning routine, actually checking the calendar and resisting the urge to let clutter creep back in – you free up mental space and time. And what's the biggest reward? More time for the fun stuff. Whether it's spending time with the kids or sneaking in a solo coffee break, discipline lets you create space for what you really enjoy. So, embrace the boring – it's the gateway to the fun!

Lunchboxes and Mealtimes

Welcome to a world where lunchboxes aren't a daily struggle and mealtimes don't feel like a battle zone! In this chapter you'll find some simple, tasty and nutritious lunchbox and meal ideas that won't break the bank or require a chef's skills to complete. There are easy-to-follow tips for reducing food-shopping costs and planning meals ahead, plus new recipes to try, so you don't feel like you're forever in culinary Groundhog Week.

You'll discover how to make mealtimes and lunchboxes fun and exciting so your kids actually eat what you pack – no more untouched sandwiches or sneaky veggie avoidance. With a mix of smart budgeting, clever prep strategies and creative twists to keep meals interesting, you'll turn chaos into calm and put the joy back into family meals. Whether you're dealing with picky eaters or just looking to simplify your routine, this guide will help you plan, prep and conquer mealtimes like a pro.

BATCH COOKING

Children are often picky eaters, and it's easy to fall into the trap of cooking the same meals every week – because, let's face it, it's less stressful than trying to convince them to try new foods. Who needs the fight? But why not make life even easier by batch cooking their favourite dishes? Prepare double (or perhaps quadruple) portions, then divide and freeze them for those hectic days when you're short on time and need to reclaim a few precious minutes.

For instance, blueberry muffins (or chocolate if you're feeling naughty) are perfect for bulk baking and freezing. They make a quick, healthy breakfast that you can just pop in the microwave for a warm treat before school or nursery. Kids love them, and let's be honest, so do adults! Whether it's a dinner or breakfast solution, batch cooking can save you time, reduce stress and make mealtimes easier for everyone in the family.

LUNCHBOX TRICKS

Every mum knows that packed lunches are the work of the devil, and it's doubly infuriating when they come home untouched. By making your children's lunchboxes more exciting, they're far more likely to indulge.

Swap the same old sandwich for wraps, mini bagels or homemade pizza slices. Add some fun by cutting sandwiches into shapes using cookie cutters, because a star-shaped sandwich is instantly cooler than a square one.

Next, include bite-sized fruits and veggies like carrot sticks, cucumber slices or pieces of pineapple. Add a dip like hummus or yoghurt for a little extra fun. Finally, try adding a surprise treat – a small note or stickers can go a long way.

Once you've got a few ideas, why not create a lunch planner that you stick to each week? This way you don't need to dream up new meal ideas but can still keep it fresh, meaning your little ones won't get bored and there is far less chance of the lunch ending up in the bin! See page 65 for more lunchbox ideas.

FIVE-MINUTE HEALTHY MEALS

Some days, for all the will in the world, you just run out of time. For the days where you feel like you're running up the down escalator, here are five super-quick, five-minute healthy meal ideas that are nutritious, tasty and will give you the energy to keep going.

- **Avocado toast with egg**: Toast some wholegrain bread, smash half an avocado on top and sprinkle with salt, pepper and a drizzle of olive oil. Fry or poach an egg, then place it on the avocado. It's packed with protein, fibre and healthy fats to keep you full and energized.

- **Greek yoghurt and berry parfait**: Layer Greek yoghurt with a handful of mixed berries and a sprinkle of granola or nuts. Add a drizzle of honey or a pinch of cinnamon for extra flavour. This meal is rich in protein, antioxidants and healthy carbs – perfect for breakfast or a snack.

- **Veggie stir-fry wrap**: Heat up a wholewheat wrap, then stir-fry pre-chopped veggies (like peppers, carrots and spinach) in olive oil with a dash of soy sauce or balsamic vinegar. Add hummus or shredded cheese, roll it up and you've got a quick, nutrient-packed meal. If you are a meat lover, throw in some leftover roast chicken, or add chilli if you like a kick.

- **Tuna and avocado salad**: Mix a can of tuna with diced avocado, a squeeze of lemon juice, salt, pepper and a bit of olive oil. Serve it over a bed of spinach or mixed greens for a simple, protein-packed meal with healthy fats. You can eat it as a salad or wrap it in lettuce leaves for a low-carb option.

- **Smoothie power bowl**: Blend a smoothie with frozen berries, banana, a handful of spinach and some almond milk. Pour it into a bowl and top with granola, chia seeds and more fresh fruit. This is a fun, refreshing and fibre-rich meal loaded with vitamins and nutrients, great for breakfast or a snack.

REDUCING FOOD COSTS

Reducing food costs doesn't mean surviving on instant noodles and toast. First, try shopping online (see page 51). Staying away from the supermarket makes it easier to resist the temptation of those buy-one-get-one-free deals on things you never actually needed in the first place – allowing you to keep much greater control over your spending.

Buy in bulk, especially for staples like rice, pasta and beans. Channel your inner grandma and embrace leftovers – transform last night's roast chicken into today's stir-fry. Also, skip the fancy brands. Generic cereal is most likely made in the same factory as the branded stuff, costs much less and tastes just as good (and your kids won't even know the difference).

Lastly, if you're going to visit a grocery store, don't do it while hungry. Everything looks gourmet when you're starving and that's how you end up buying a trolley full of kids' party food. A little planning goes a long way in keeping your purse happy and your sugar intake in check.

FUSSY EATERS

Getting younger kids to eat dinner can feel like a negotiation with a tiny, stubborn dictator who just declared they "don't like food". But don't worry – there are tricks to winning this ridiculous battle.

First, rename everything and suddenly it's an adventure. Broccoli? Nope, that's a "Miniature Tree". Carrots? They're "X-ray Vision Sticks". Watch those veggies disappear.

Reverse psychology is also your friend. "This chicken is only for grown-ups." Oh really? They're suddenly demanding it like it's forbidden treasure.

And let's not forget the magic of dipping sauces. Ketchup, mayo, pesto, hummus – kids will eat anything if they can dip it. Even vegetables look appetizing to kids when they're doused in sauce.

Lastly, throw in the age-old trick of ~~bribery~~ "positive reinforcement". A brownie for eating all the green stuff? Sure, why not? You're not above a little dessert diplomacy if it saves you from starting a world war.

NO-COOK MEALS

Mums often feel unnecessarily guilty if they're not producing a hot meal every single day of the week. You don't need to spend hours sweating over the oven (or microwaving your electricity bill) when you could be enjoying a quick, tasty meal that requires zero cooking. Think of all the energy you'll save. Here are four mouthwatering no-cook meal ideas that'll leave you feeling satisfied and smug about your energy efficiency.

- **Charcuterie board**: Throw some cooked or cured meats, cheeses, crackers and fruit onto a board. You've got yourself a spread that looks impressive, kids love finger food and there's the added bonus that there is minimal washing-up to be done at the end. Result.

- **Mango chutney chicken sliders**: Fill some large wholemeal rolls with some shredded rotisserie chicken, red onion, chilli and salad (maybe leave out the chilli for the kids – unless you want a giggle of course!). Mix some mint sauce with Greek yoghurt for a delicious dressing and serve with a bowl of mango chutney. Kids go mad for this easy meal, and you will too.

- **Fajitas**: Kids love this one as they can build their own. Just lay out some wholemeal wraps and bowls of deli pre-cooked vegetables, avocado pieces, pre-cooked chicken, fibre-rich pinto beans and a jar of salsa.
- **Poke bowls**: The poke bowl is like the ultimate summer salad, and it's so quick to make. There are a gazillion versions of this meal online so you can change it up as much as you like. Perhaps some prawns, chickpeas or edamame beans, served with rice, sliced radish, chopped avocado, spring onions, chopped mango, a tasty dressing – whatever you think will go down well.

And don't forget, by going the no-cook route, you can use your energy-saving money to treat yourself to dessert. Just make sure you hide it so the kids don't get there first.

COOKING CLASSES

Kids are way more likely to eat when they've had a hand in the prep. By getting them involved in the kitchen, you're encouraging them to love cooking, they're kept occupied and you get to spend some quality time with your brood.

Consider signing your kids up for some cooking classes. While they can be pricey, they're a fantastic way to bond while learning new skills together – and they double as a fun outing. If you're strapped for cash, simply teach your children how to cook one of their favourite recipes at home. Arrange all the ingredients into little bowls, throw an apron on them and get them to respond to all your instructions with "Yes, Chef!" They'll love the interaction with you and by the time they're teenagers, you'll have them cooking dinner for you.

MORE LUNCHBOX TRICKS

Packed lunches are never going to be anything other than a painful slog, but these tips will hopefully make life a little easier.

- **Freeze juice cartons overnight**: They act as ice packs, keeping food cold and refreshing until lunchtime.

- **Containers with compartments**: These are a game-changer. No more hunting for tiny containers or dealing with a mountain of dishes later – just one box and you're done!

- **Leftovers from dinner**: Recycling these can save a serious chunk of time. Cold pesto pasta or last night's stir-fry? Toss it in, and there you go – instant lunch.

- **Prepare sandwich fillings in bulk**: Prepping sandwich fillings each evening can be a pain in the proverbial, so why not opt for things you can batch make instead? Tuna and egg mayo last in the fridge for at least three days if sealed. Veggie fillings like falafel and chickpeas last a lot longer still, and mixed with a sauce such as barbecue, sweet chilli or soy yoghurt, they will disappear in no time.

TEN-MINUTE GOURMET DINING (YES, REALLY!)

If you like lamb and have a slow cooker, this dish is to die for, despite the minimal time it takes to prepare – it is cooked over 8 hours, but with only 10 minutes of actual effort.

Lamb legs are amazing but they cost as much as a small mortgage. Enter lamb shanks – cheaper, just as delicious and perfect for when you want to feel fancy without breaking the bank. (If lamb isn't your thing, it takes no time to put together a delicious vegetable casserole in the slow cooker with whatever you have to hand – courgettes, peppers, tinned butterbeans or chickpeas – look online for inspiration.)

To feed four hungry humans, simply throw four lamb shanks into your trusty slow cooker. Add a pint of lamb stock, half a bottle of red wine and a couple of tablespoons of mint sauce. That's it. No browning, no faffing, no stress. Set the slow cooker to low, walk away for 8 hours and revel in the fact that you've just completed all your cooking duties for the day in about 5 minutes flat. Time to kick back and read a book... or take a nap. (Maybe that's too much to ask for!)

By the time dinner rolls around, your home will smell like heaven – or at least a really posh restaurant. Five minutes before you're ready to eat, simply nuke some boiled potatoes and microwave a selection of pre-cut veg. Take the lamb shanks out of the slow cooker, skim the fat off the sauce like a professional chef (ladle in hand, looking smug), then pour the remaining liquid into a frying pan. Reduce it down to a thick, glossy jus that will make you look like you spent hours slaving away.

And there you have it – a gourmet dinner that's so easy, you'll almost feel guilty accepting the inevitable praise. Almost.

ENERGY BALL GOODNESS

Energy balls are the new black. These little snacks are the ultimate "I'm pretending to be a supermum" trick. They're easy to make, healthy and sneak in all the good stuff your kids would usually feed to the dog.

To whip up some sneaky chocolate orange energy balls that your kids will think are a treat, just blitz 100 g of pitted medjool dates, 100 g pecans, 50 g pumpkin seeds, 50 g oats and 4 tablespoons of cocoa powder in a food processor. Add 2 heaped tablespoons of maple syrup, plus the zest and juice of one orange, then blend again until it forms a sticky dough. Roll into bite-sized balls and refrigerate. They'll taste like a chocolatey dessert, but they're secretly full of goodness!

You can even make a large batch ahead of time and simply freeze until you need them. Just pop them in your kids' lunchboxes and they'll be defrosted by noon.

REDUCING FOOD WASTE

Reducing food waste can be easy and fun, simply by getting creative with what you already have in your fridge and cupboards. Instead of tossing out ingredients, write them down and search on the internet for recipe ideas. You'll be amazed at the number of dishes you can create with those random items – like that tin of butterbeans which has been sat in the same spot for who knows how long, gathering dust. You can get your kids involved too and see who can come up with the best ideas, with a small prize for the winner.

This approach not only prevents waste but also helps you discover new recipes and cooking techniques. You might find a delicious stew, salad or dip you'd never have thought to make otherwise. It's a win for your purse, your cooking skills and the environment!

BAKED POTATO IDEAS

Baked potatoes are a cheap, versatile and filling meal option that can be quickly prepared, making them a great staple in any kitchen. Simply prick them all over with a fork and microwave for 6–7 minutes, finishing them off for 15 minutes in the oven at 200°C/gas mark 6 or 5 minutes in an air fryer. If you're not fussed about them being crispy, you can microwave the whole thing in 8 minutes on days you're strapped for time (or your kids won't stop whining that they're *starving*).

Classic choices include butter, cheese, beans, sour cream or tuna, but the options are endless. For a healthier twist without the extra calories, try topping them with steamed vegetables, cottage cheese or tomato salsa for added flavour.

Any leftover baked potatoes can also be easily repurposed. You can create delicious crispy wedges for the following day with minimal fuss. Simply cut your leftover potatoes lengthways into quarters, toss them in a little oil and bake in the oven at 200°C/gas mark 6 for about 15 minutes. These wedges turn out crispy and golden, perfect as a side or snack. They're a blank canvas, ready to be topped with cheese, chilli, sour cream, guacamole, crispy bacon or even sprinkled with herbs and spices for added flavour.

They are also a great base for heartier meals. Pile them high with pulled pork, shredded chicken or a veggie chilli for a satisfying, balanced dish. If you're feeling adventurous, add a drizzle of barbecue sauce or melted cheese for extra indulgence.

The humble baked potato not only saves money but also allows you to get creative with toppings and leftovers, reducing waste and keeping mealtimes exciting. It's a simple yet brilliant way to stretch your ingredients and fill hungry bellies, without costing a fortune.

ONE-POT WONDERS

One-pot meals are a lifesaver. Here are four tasty recipes to save you precious time.

- **Chilli con (or non) carne**: Yes, it's a bit boring, but most kids love it and sometimes the old favourites are the best. Everything cooks in one pot, from the beef or veggie mince to the kidney beans, leaving you with nothing but flavour. For four people, start by browning 500 g of minced beef, or the manufacturer's recommended equivalent of veggie mince, in a large pot. Add a chopped onion and two cloves of minced garlic, and fry until soft. Stir in two cans of diced tomatoes, one tin of kidney beans, a chopped green pepper, half a pint of beef or veggie stock and two teaspoons of chilli powder, then let it simmer for about 30 minutes. Make extra to freeze for a quick meal another day.

- **Chicken alfredo pasta**: For this gorgeous creamy dish just fry some diced chicken and add three cloves of chopped garlic and 300 ml of double cream. Simmer for 5–10 mins until the cream thickens, add 50 g of parmesan and some cooked pasta. You can even add a little chilli if you're feeling spicy. Serve with garlic bread. (Okay, so this isn't strictly one-pot, but it is delicious!)

- **Stir-fry noodles**: Fry everything in one wok – it's fast, furious and mess-free. Heat a little oil and stir-fry your choice of protein (chicken, prawns or tofu) for a few minutes. Add vegetables (like peppers and broccoli) and cook until tender. Toss in pre-cooked noodles and your favourite sauce, stir-frying for an additional 3–5 minutes.

- **Beef stew**: For a cosy winter meal, peel and chop potatoes, carrots and onions, then add them to a slow cooker with 500 g–1 kg of diced beef, stock and seasoning. Cook on low for 6–8 hours or high for 3–4 hours until tender. If using the oven, cook at 160°C/gas mark 3 for 4 hours.

THEMED EVENINGS

If you're tired of cooking the same meals week after week and feel like you're stuck in a culinary rut, why not try mixing things up by introducing themed food nights? Keeping a routine but adding variety makes meal planning more exciting, without the stress of starting from scratch every week. For example, Monday could be Mexican night – think tacos, enchiladas or fajitas. Tuesday could be Italian night with pasta, pizza or risotto. You can easily adapt this for other cuisines like Asian, Mediterranean or French.

Food-themed evenings are also a great way to get the kids involved in meal planning and cooking. For younger children, let them help you choose the theme and brainstorm meal ideas. For older kids, encourage them to research dishes online that fit the theme. It's a fun way for them to learn about different cuisines and become more invested in what they eat.

For teenagers, give them one night a week to take charge of cooking. They can choose a recipe that suits their skill level – simple dishes like stir-fries, pasta or quesadillas are great starting points. This not only teaches them a valuable life skill but also builds their confidence in the kitchen. Plus, they'll take pride in creating something the whole family can enjoy together (and you get a well-deserved night off cooking).

Themed food nights break the monotony of routine, making mealtimes something to look forward to while giving your kids a sense of responsibility and creativity. It's a great way to teach them about food, cooking and culture, all while making the week's meals feel fresh and fun. And who knows? You might discover some new family favourites along the way!

FUSSY EATERS – ADVANCED TACTICS

If you've mastered the basics of fussy-eating tactics, it's time to level up to the *advanced* course. Enter the lockable treat box. This strategy takes "eat your vegetables, get a treat" to a whole new level. Here's how it works: Get a small lockable box, secure it with a four-digit code and put your kid's favourite snack inside. Now, for every few mouthfuls of vegetables they choke down, they get to unlock one number of the combination.

We challenge even the pickiest of eaters to resist the urge of unlocking that treat box. Plus, it adds a layer of excitement that transforms dinner into a top-secret mission. Who knew spinach could be so thrilling? This is a great way to get dinner time boxed off quickly, without the 30-minute fight. Just make sure you get a box with a digital code you can change daily – or else you'll need to purchase 10,000 padlocks!

GUILT-FREE TAKE-OUT

If you're really strapped for time and can't even manage a no-cook meal, take-out is here to save the day! Of course, ordering-in is expensive, but occasionally it's nice to treat yourself. And it doesn't have to be a calorie-heavy meal either.

Take chicken shish kebabs, for example. Order them with a fresh salad, skip the chips and you've got a protein-packed, veggie-filled meal that tastes like a treat but won't wreck your diet. Or go for a tomato-based curry with rice – light on the cream, heavy on the flavour. It's warm, satisfying and still relatively healthy. Sushi is another excellent option. Fresh fish or avocado, rice and seaweed? Yes, please! Just maybe go easy on the fried vegetable tempura.

Remember, even take-out can be a guilt-free, time-saving hero if you make smart choices. So go ahead – let someone else cook and pat yourself on the back for ordering wisely.

Easy Self-Care Wins

Hopefully you're now feeling super organized and confident about applying the tips and hacks from the previous chapter to free up valuable time to focus on yourself. It's easy to feel overwhelmed by life's demands, but creating time for self-care is essential to maintaining your well-being. Start by learning to say no to less important things and instead assign time in your planner that's dedicated just to you.

Self-care doesn't need to be a grand event or require lavish equipment – it can be practised in small, meaningful ways throughout the day. Simple acts, like enjoying a cup of tea in peace or taking a 10-minute walk, are micro self-care moments that can make a big difference. Meanwhile, more substantial self-care rituals, such as going for a run or attending a weekly class, provide deeper relaxation and fulfilment. In this chapter, you'll find practical ideas to help you nurture yourself, no matter how busy life gets.

GUILT-FREE SELF-CARE

For busy mums, saying "no" to requests or tasks that are not mandatory is crucial to creating time for self-care. It's easy to feel guilted into constantly spinning multiple plates but saying "yes" to every request can leave you feeling exhausted and burned out. Prioritizing your own needs is essential for your well-being, allowing you to recharge and be more present for your family. Self-care is not selfish. Nor is it something you should feel guilty about.

One way to reclaim time is by blocking out specific self-care slots in your diary, treating them like any other important appointment. You can also delegate tasks, say "no" to extra commitments or simplify your schedule by using a digital calendar (see pages 42–43). By being selective about where your energy goes, you'll find that carving out time for yourself becomes more achievable – and everyone benefits when Mum is recharged and refreshed, especially your kids. See? You're doing them a favour!

Self-care isn't selfish; it's essential for maintaining balance and well-being.

DIGITAL DETOX

Let's face it, mums, the digital world is like a clingy toddler – it never gives you a moment's peace. Between emails that ding louder than your alarm clock and social media feeds that make you feel guilty for not making gluten-free, organic unicorn toast, it's no wonder we're frazzled. Enter the glorious concept of the digital detox, where you can reclaim your sanity one unplugged moment at a time. Put those pesky school WhatsApp groups on silent, turn your data off when you need to focus and set a designated time period each day for replying to emails and messages. Make a habit of setting aside a regular time when you will do something that doesn't involve technology. Leave your phone at home when you go for that walk. Taking a break from the digital madness lets you reconnect with the real world – like, you know, your actual kids.

THE IMPORTANCE OF SLEEP

For mums, getting a good night's sleep isn't just a luxury – it's a survival tactic. When you're running on fumes, everything feels harder and it's much easier to make mistakes. Those "why is my phone in the fridge?" moments happen a little too often, and suddenly your child's school project feels like you're building the next space shuttle.

Create a calming bedtime routine by disconnecting from screens at least an hour before bed and keep your bedroom cool and dark for better sleep quality. Prioritize consistency by going to bed and waking up at the same time every day, even on weekends. Sticking to a consistent sleep schedule not only helps you fall asleep faster but also boosts your overall health by improving your memory, mood and immune function.

Lack of sleep also contributes to a reduction in skin collagen production and increases your wrinkles! So, skip the expensive Botox, embrace the satisfaction of saying "goodnight" and enjoy a few extra hours of much-needed, well-deserved shut-eye.

MICRO SELF-CARE

Finding time for self-care can be tough, but it doesn't have to be a huge commitment. With micro self-care, you can fit rejuvenating activities into even the busiest days. Here are five quick self-care ideas that take just a few minutes.

- **Mini meditation** (5 minutes): Sit or lie somewhere comfortable, close your eyes, take deep breaths and focus on each inhale and exhale. A short meditation can help clear your mind, reduce stress and restore calm.

- **Stretch break** (3 minutes): Step away from your desk or daily chores and do a few simple stretches, focusing on your whole body. Loosen your muscles, release tension and get your blood flowing for an instant energy boost.

- **Gratitude journalling** (5 minutes): Take a moment to jot down three things you're grateful for. This quick practice shifts your mindset, helps you appreciate the positive and fosters emotional well-being.

- **Cup of tea in silence** (10 minutes): Brew your favourite tea and enjoy it without distractions. This brief pause allows you to unwind, refocus and have a peaceful moment to yourself.

- **Listen to your favourite song** (4 minutes): Put on a song that makes you feel good and just listen. Music has the power to elevate your mood and transport you out of the stress of the day, even if just for a few minutes.

These micro self-care activities can fit into any schedule, helping you take short but meaningful breaks to recharge. Whether it's buying yourself some flowers, taking a walk to clear your mind or getting up early to watch the sunrise, these small moments can have a big impact on your mental and emotional health. They're a simple reminder that taking care of yourself doesn't always require a lot of time – just a little intention.

MAKE A VISION BOARD

Creating a vision board is a powerful act of self-care because it helps you reconnect with your personal goals, dreams and values. As a mum, it's easy to get wrapped up in your children's needs, often at the expense of your own. A vision board shifts your focus back to what's important to *you*, allowing you to identify *your* desires and aspirations. By seeing visual representations of your goals, you have a lovely daily reminder of what you want to achieve, inspiring small but meaningful actions.

To make a vision board, start with a cork board, drawing pins and magazines or printouts with inspiring images and words. Reflect on your goals, dreams and values in areas like career, health, relationships or personal growth. Cut out images, quotes and affirmations that represent these aspirations and simply arrange them on the board. Place your vision board somewhere visible as a daily reminder to stay focused on the things that matter to you most.

YOU CANNOT
SERVE FROM AN
EMPTY VESSEL.

Eleanor Brownn

POWER OF PLANTS

Gardening is a great way to spend some time in the fresh air, but did you know that being green-fingered can actually change how you feel? Many horticulturists will tell you that gardening brings a sense of joy and well-being to their lives and there are a great deal of studies that suggest this peaceful activity has significant benefits for your mental health. Research in Japan found that simply looking at plants can reduce stress, anger and sadness. Similarly, a study by the UK charity Mind showed that short walks in gardens can boost mental health and mood.

The physical act of tending to plants creates a sense of accomplishment and calm and the mindfulness of gardening encourages you to live in the present. Whether planting flowers, potting windowsill herbs, caring for houseplants or growing vegetables, gardening can be a therapeutic escape from daily stress, promoting both mental and emotional well-being.

DOLCE FAR NIENTE

Dolce far niente is an Italian phrase that translates to "the sweetness of doing nothing". However, this mantra is not about being idle or wasting time. The essence of this message is to take a moment to savour life's simple pleasures. As a busy mum, this concept is vital. Often, there's an expectation and invisible pressure to constantly be doing something – taking care of the household, the kids or work. But *dolce far niente* reminds us that it's okay to pause, enjoy the quiet moments and take a breath – and is the perfect antidote to your time-sucking *piccoli diavoli* (little devils!).

In today's fast-paced world, we're often caught up in constant productivity, leaving barely any room for moments of rest or reflection. It's okay, and even beneficial, to slow down and enjoy idleness. Whether it's listening to birdsong, watching the sunset or simply daydreaming, embracing these moments of stillness can rejuvenate the mind and soul.

Easy Self-Care Wins

GO BIG ON SELF-CARE

Carving out time for bigger self-care rituals can feel like an elusive dream. But these moments are golden and give you the chance to recharge beyond the usual quick fixes. Here are five self-care ideas that might just make you feel like a human again – no kids, no laundry, just you.

- **Go for a run** (30–45 minutes): Whether it's a light jog or a full sprint, getting out for a run clears your mind and gets your body moving. Plus, it's one of the few times where "running away" is totally acceptable!

- **Meet a friend for coffee** (sans kids, of course) (1 hour): Remember adult conversation? Grab a coffee (and a slice of cake, obviously) with a friend and actually talk about things other than homework, snack requests or *Paw Patrol*. It's like a mini holiday for your brain.

- **Take an evening class** (1–2 hours): Sign up for something you love, whether it's pottery, dance or learning a new language. It's an opportunity to do something just for you and rekindle old passions – or discover new ones.

- **Spa morning/afternoon or DIY spa at home** (1–3 hours): If you can escape to a spa, fantastic. If not, bring the spa home. Light candles, play some relaxing music, take a long bath, do a face mask and just be…

- **Weekend hike or nature walk** (2–3 hours): Get out in nature, soak up some fresh air and clear your head with a hike or leisurely walk. It's exercise and relaxation all in one, and nobody will ask you to tie their shoes or use the word "mum" 50,000 times.

These bigger self-care moments are your chance to recharge, reconnect and reclaim your sanity – one child-free hour at a time.

BE KIND TO YOURSELF

We often focus on what we haven't accomplished rather than celebrating what we've achieved. It's essential to practise self-compassion and forgiveness, especially on those days when everything seems to be going wrong: a bad night's sleep, laundry piling up or dishes left undone. Instead of letting these frustrations take over, talk to yourself like a friend instead of an enemy and let go of the idea that anyone or anything is perfect. We all have off days and even weeks. For those days where you just can't seem to let that inner critic go, try using a meditation app to get outside of your own thoughts.

Studies have shown that using meditation apps can reduce emotional reactivity, negative feelings and shift your focus toward the positive steps you've taken, no matter how small. Even one or two small acts of kindness toward yourself can have a profound impact on your mood, helping you feel more balanced and ready to tackle the day with renewed energy.

Taking time for yourself today creates a stronger version of you tomorrow.

THERAPY

Sometimes, the most powerful form of self-care is recognizing when life has become too overwhelming and acknowledging that you might need professional help. In a world that often emphasizes the importance of self-reliance, especially for mums, it can feel difficult to admit that you're struggling. Mums are often expected to be the spinner of all plates and make navigating life look easy. News flash – it's not! Seeking help from a therapist for treatment such as Cognitive Behavioural Therapy (CBT) or counselling is not a sign of weakness; it's a courageous and proactive step toward improving your mental well-being. You can get a referral by going to your doctor or look online for self-referral CBT or counselling in your area.

CBT is a highly effective therapeutic approach with numerous benefits. It focuses on identifying and challenging negative thought patterns that contribute to feelings of anxiety, depression or stress. By helping you reframe these thoughts and replace them with healthier, more constructive perspectives, CBT empowers you to take control of your emotional and mental state. Over time, you learn skills that allow you to cope more effectively with challenges, manage stress and reduce the risk of spiralling into overwhelming emotional states.

CBT is solution-focused and equips you with tools to manage your current circumstances and foster resilience for the future. Just as you would seek medical attention for a broken bone, taking care of your mental health is no less essential.

When you're mentally in control, it's far easier to manage your time effectively. Once you finish therapy, not only will you be better equipped to handle life in general, but you'll also be in a routine of carving out an hour a week to talk to a professional. Why not keep it going and use the same hour each week to indulge in another act of self-care? You will be able to enjoy it much more when you're feeling at peace with yourself.

CRYING

Although it might seem surprising, giving yourself permission to cry can be incredibly therapeutic and beneficial for your body. Rather than bottling up emotions, shedding tears allows for a natural release and promotes emotional healing. Historically, in ancient Greece and Rome, tears were believed to cleanse and purify the soul, symbolizing both strength and renewal. Today, science confirms the benefits of crying, as it triggers the release of oxytocin and endorphins – hormones that enhance feelings of well-being and reduce stress.

Crying is not a sign of weakness but rather a powerful tool for self-soothing and emotional processing. In fact, embracing this vulnerability can help you restore emotional balance and foster a deeper sense of clarity. If you don't cry easily, you can always watch an emotional movie – even if you start crying over something completely unrelated to you, the effect is just as cathartic.

WHEN A WOMAN
BECOMES HER
OWN BEST FRIEND,
LIFE IS EASIER.

Diane von Fürstenberg

DITCH THE MORNING NEWS

Reaching for your phone first thing in the morning, especially to check the news, can adversely impact your mental health. Most news articles focus on negative events – disasters, conflicts and crises – which can set a seriously gloomy tone for your day. When you start your morning reading about everything wrong in the world, it reinforces a sense that not only is your life tough, but the planet is falling apart too. This mindset can leave you feeling overwhelmed, anxious and unmotivated before you've even started your day.

Instead, a great act of self-care is to take a break from the news in the morning and try something more positive, such as practising mindfulness, stretching or reading a book of inspirational quotes. Starting your day with uplifting content can set a positive tone, help you feel more in control and give you the energy to tackle challenges with a clearer, more optimistic mindset.

WRITE A LETTER TO FUTURE YOU

Take a moment to grab a pen and paper and write a letter to your future self. This could be for you to read in one, two or even five years' time. In the letter, express your hopes, dreams and the challenges you're currently facing. Reflect on the lessons you've learned along the way. It's an empowering exercise that allows you to pause and think about your personal growth while setting intentions for the future. You might also consider writing a letter to your children, capturing your life lessons and updating it as they grow.

Looking back on these letters is a great way to see how much you've evolved. After all, time is precious, and this is a great reminder that the actions you take now will determine where you are in the future.

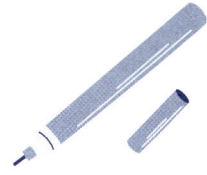

Easy Self-Care Wins

EXERCISE WITHOUT THE "URGH" FACTOR

We all know that exercise is an excellent form of self-care that promotes physical and mental well-being. According to the World Health Organization (WHO), engaging in regular physical activity helps prevent disease and illness, such as coronary heart disease, stroke, type 2 diabetes and cancer, maintains overall health and improves physical and mental resilience. It can also significantly increase your life expectancy.

If the idea of going for a run makes you want to go back to bed, try looking for something more fun and engaging in your local area. Aerial silks and pole dancing classes provide full-body workouts that enhance flexibility and strength while feeling more like fun social events than traditional workouts. Barre classes, which combine ballet-inspired moves with core-focused exercises, are another great option. For those with little ones or pets, baby yoga and doggy yoga (doga) classes are enjoyable alternatives to everyday activities, allowing you to combine bonding time with physical fitness.

If you're strapped for cash, why not bring the class to you? Get a few mum friends over and find a YouTube yoga class. There are stacks of them online to choose from. You could even invest in your own pole and take over the living room! It's a great way to save time by combining a social activity with exercise and with the added bonus that you don't need to find the time to go to the gym.

SELF-CARE SPENDING

Treating yourself is important, but let's be frank – fun activities can be really expensive! Why not make finding funds for your next treat a little easier? Start a simple savings plan and reward yourself when you hit your goal. You could go old-school and toss your spare change into a jar until it adds up or, for a modern twist, use a handy banking tool that saves for you. Most banks offer an account that "rounds up" each transaction to the nearest pound, transferring the difference to a savings account. You'll be surprised at how quickly the savings grow – without you even noticing. Set a fun goal, like saving for a spa day or an adrenaline-pumping theme-park trip. After all, what's better than guilt-free fun you've earned with your own savings?

Don't waste time worrying about the future. Every problem has an end date. Every future trouble will eventually become an issue of the past.

THE "18 MINUTES A DAY" RULE

The "18 minutes a day" rule is a powerful way to study something new and become better than 95 per cent of the world in that discipline. The idea originates from Josh Kaufman's book *The First 20 Hours,* which suggests that 18 minutes' practice in any discipline every day can lead to significant proficiency in a new skill.

Most of us waste many hours a week scrolling through social media or watching random videos – so why not use that time to develop a new and valuable skill? Try learning to play an instrument like the ukulele, or take up something fun and energetic like street dancing. Imagine jamming out on a guitar, using code or chatting with someone in French. There are countless free tutorials on YouTube and other streaming services, so it doesn't need to break the bank. This is a great way to utilize a small amount of time, to achieve something you can be really proud of.

LAUGH!

Who doesn't love to laugh? The great news is that not only is laughter fun, it also has a shed load of benefits for both your mind and body. Research shows that, a lot like crying, social laughter releases endorphins – our brain's feel-good hormones – promoting a sense of well-being and happiness. A good laugh doesn't just lift your mood; it strengthens relationships by creating shared moments of joy and connection. Whether you're sharing a joke with friends or enjoying a comedy show, laughter builds bonds that deepen emotional closeness.

Though laughter isn't something you can force, you can put yourself in situations that spark it, like watching a funny movie or going to a comedy club. A fun mums' night out, filled with giggles and jokes, can be just what you need to unwind and feel good. Beyond just brightening your day, laughter lowers stress, boosts your immune system and even eases tension. It truly is nature's best medicine – free, contagious and endlessly fun!

HELP YOURSELF BY HELPING OTHERS

An act of self-care doesn't have to focus solely on personal well-being. Volunteering can give us a sense of purpose, boosting self-esteem and reducing feelings of loneliness. Studies have shown that people who suffer from anxiety can benefit from volunteering, which can reduce stress and increase feelings of positivity and relaxation due to a spike in dopamine. Similarly, for those struggling with depression, one of the most effective ways to give yourself a lift is by helping others. This is because giving brings a deeper sense of joy than focusing solely on yourself. Here are a few ideas to get you started.

- **School involvement**: Volunteering at school, such as helping with PTA events, organizing fundraisers or assisting in classrooms, allows you to contribute to your child's education while staying engaged with the local community.

- **Charity shops or food banks**: Volunteering at a local charity shop or food bank offers flexible hours and the chance to give back to those in need. These roles are often family-friendly and can be a great way to teach kids about helping others.

- **Meal delivery for the elderly**: Delivering meals to elderly neighbours or families in need is a thoughtful way to provide support. This can be organized through community groups or meal-sharing networks, offering practical help to those who may be struggling.

- **Sports coaching or mentoring**: If you have a passion for sports or a specific skill, coaching or mentoring in local youth programmes can be a rewarding way to volunteer. This provides positive role models for children and can be a great way to stay active while contributing to the community.

There are loads of different ways you can get involved with your local community. Have a look on your local area social media pages for more ideas and give your own mood a lovely boost by helping others.

Making Memories

You've now seen how prioritizing your own needs can revitalize you, leaving you feeling happier and giving you a well-deserved break. Once you've restored your energy, you'll also be more emotionally present for your kids. Having filled your own cup, it's time to focus on creating meaningful, fun moments with the rest of the family.

This chapter will dive into why play is so important for bonding and how it helps you connect with your kids. You'll learn how to live in the moment, let go and lose yourself in play – no, it doesn't involve pretending to be a dinosaur or princess for the hundredth time!

There will also be fun, simple activities you can do together – indoors, outdoors and with zero spending. From baking with little helpers to creative games for older ones, there's something for all ages. Keep reading and learn how to make the most of that precious family time.

DITCH THE PHONE

These days, everyone seems to be hooked to their phones like they're some form of life-support machine. As if you didn't already know, an increasing number of studies suggest that phones are highly addictive, so who can blame you? Maybe the phone companies make them that way on purpose – so you don't realize that the constant digital connection is robbing you of something far more important: time for real play with your kids.

Whether you're crawling around on your hands and knees (not the best way to get carpet burns) or assembling the 1,000-piece Lego deathtrap you will inevitably step on later, playtime can be tough when you're feeling tired or you're particularly busy. But listen – ditching your phone can turn playtime into something surprisingly fun.

The key is letting go. Yes, you're going to be bad at this. But that's the fun of it! Kids don't care if you're awkward at pretend play or can't quite roar like a lion. What they'll remember is that you were there, present, fully engaged – no phone in sight.

And who knows? You might actually enjoy a game of hide and seek more than doom-scrolling social media. Taking time away from your phone will also show your kids that it's not *essential* and doesn't need to be viewed constantly, and if you value being in the moment more than using your devices, so will they.

STORY STONES

Storytelling is a powerful way to nurture a child's imagination, foster creativity and strengthen communication skills. But if you'd rather slam your head against the wall than read your kid's favourite story for the sixtieth time, try making some story stones. All you need is 12 smooth pebbles and some acrylic paint pens, then draw simple pictures on each side, such as animals, stars or houses – let your imagination run wild. Once painted, spray them with varnish to preserve the designs, and store them in a hessian drawstring bag.

This is a great (cheap) homemade gift for a birthday or Christmas and a lasting source of imaginative play. Every night, your children can take one stone (or more) from the bag and use the images to create new stories. The tactile and visual nature of story stones sparks creative thinking, offering hours of storytelling fun, while also building memories and bonding time together for the whole family.

Be present in the moment – it's the little everyday things that your children will carry with them for a lifetime.

MOVIE MAGIC

An indoor movie night is a fantastic way to combine family time with fun, turn an ordinary evening into something memorable and stay cosy at home. All you need is a TV, a comfy space with pillows and blankets and your kids' favourite movie. Let them help set the scene with dim lighting, or fairy lights for a magical touch, and whip up some homemade popcorn – just toss kernels and a little oil in a pan with a lid, then heat until they pop. You could even serve pick-and-mix sweets in individual paper bags.

The best part? It's not just about the movie – it's about spending uninterrupted time together. With everyone snuggled up and away from distractions, you'll find it easier to connect. It's a simple yet special way to create lasting memories, transforming a regular night into a cinematic adventure without ever leaving the house – and if you do happen to have a projector, you could easily take movie night outside to the garden, under the stars!

DIY ESCAPE ROOMS

Escape rooms are brilliant fun – until you see the price and realize you're paying to be locked in a room with your own children. So why not bring that excitement (and chaos) home? Start by picking a theme (pirates, superheroes, space aliens – the sky's the limit), then scatter clues around the house. Use riddles, puzzles and hidden keys and padlocks to unlock boxes and doors. Give them an hour to solve all the tasks or they fail and lose their after-dinner treat (mwah ha ha).

For younger kids, keep it simple: colour-coded clues or easy tasks like "find the red sock". If they're older, you can crank up the difficulty and throw in some anagrams or mathematical puzzles, or even hide the final key inside a block of ice.

It's all the fun of an expensive escape room, without the cost – and the best part? You get to be the evil mastermind, laughing as your children race against the clock.

THERE'S NO WAY TO BE A PERFECT MOTHER AND A MILLION WAYS TO BE A GOOD ONE.

Jill Churchill

GEOCACHING

Geocaching is an adventurous and interactive way to entertain kids, sparking curiosity, problem-solving and a love for exploration. It's easy to get started and works for any age or family outing, whether it's a weekend forest walk or a trip to the park.

Begin by downloading a geocaching app and searching for caches nearby. Each cache comes with clues to help locate it, ranging from beginner-friendly hints to challenging riddles for older kids. The "treasure" might be a small trinket or a logbook to sign, and kids can even leave their own little items in return.

It's a creative, low-cost way to combine outdoor fun with teamwork and discovery – and it gets everyone off screens and into nature.

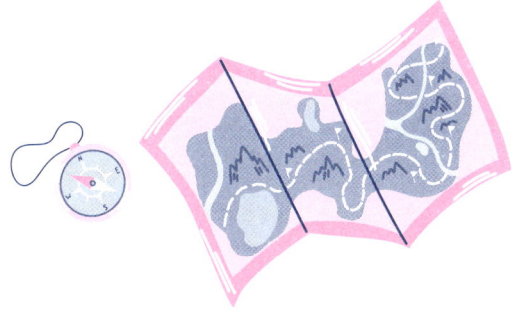

DIY SCIENCE EXPERIMENTS

DIY science experiments with your kids are a perfect way to mix learning and fun, with a side of inevitable mess, but hey, what's a little food colouring on the ceiling if it gets them excited about science? These ideas should get you started, but there are thousands more you can find by searching online.

- **Build a volcano**: The classic bicarbonate of soda and vinegar volcano never disappoints. To build a "volcano", use playdough to make the structure around an empty plastic bottle, pour in some vinegar, washing-up liquid (and red food colouring if you want to be super authentic), then let the kids add the bicarbonate of soda. A mini lava explosion will erupt immediately. Just be ready for the inevitable request to do it ten more times.

- **Invisible ink spy messages**: Mix lemon juice with a bit of water and then write secret messages on paper using cotton buds. Once dry, use a heat source (a lamp will do) to reveal the hidden writing. The best part? Watching them behave like mini detectives as they decode the mildly insulting messages you've written down (got to make it fun for Mum too, right?)

- **Magic milk**: Pour some milk into a dish, add a few drops of food colouring and let the kids touch the surface with a cotton bud dipped in washing-up liquid. The colours will burst apart like a little milk firework.

- **Homemade crystals**: To make homemade crystals, simply dissolve 1 cup of sugar or salt in 1 cup of hot water. Pour the solution into a clean jar and add a few drops of food colouring if desired. Place a string or wooden stick in the jar, and let it sit undisturbed for several days to form crystals.

These hands-on activities not only teach kids about how things work but also keep them entertained, and maybe even away from their screens for a little while. You may even learn a few new things too!

FAMILY TRADITIONS

By their very nature, traditions are consistent. Children find huge comfort in predictability, especially when times are tough. Similar to routines, the stability and continuity of family customs help children feel grounded when their world may seem uncertain or chaotic.

Family traditions don't have to be grandiose or complicated events – they can be as simple as weekly "pancake Sundays" where you end up covered in batter or a monthly movie night where you all wear pyjamas.

Family traditions give everyone something to bond over, even if the kids insist on a water balloon fight every time they finish school for the summer. Whether it's baking cookies together for birthdays or a seasonal trip to a Christmas market, it's these quirky, shared traditions that create a sense of belonging and joy. No matter how busy life gets, you always have these special moments to rely on and enjoy together as a family.

GRATITUDE LIST

Sharing a gratitude list with your children before bed is a simple yet powerful way of boosting well-being, reducing anxiety and encouraging them to be less materialistic. Each family member takes turns saying three things they're grateful for – whether it's something as basic as having food and a warm home or something personal like playing a fun game that day. This practice helps kids recognize and appreciate the good in their lives, making them more aware of the things they might otherwise take for granted, like eyesight or a cosy bed.

It's also a wonderful way to wind down, fostering a positive mindset before sleep. To take it a step further, you could keep a family journal, writing down moments from everyone's day. This not only helps everyone reflect but also becomes a cherished keepsake, capturing memories you would otherwise forget. Years later, you'll have a treasure trove of heartwarming moments to look back on.

Time won't wait for you — make the most of every moment while you can.

UNCONVENTIONAL CAMPING

Camping at home – whether in your living room or the garden – offers all the adventure without any of the hassle. No need to pack endless supplies, brave the elements or worry about creepy-crawly (unwelcome) visitors. Simply pitch a tent (or create a makeshift blanket version for indoors), grab some cosy sleeping bags and let the fun begin. You can tell stories by torchlight, toast marshmallows on the barbeque or in the oven and even stargaze if you're outdoors.

The best part? If the ground gets uncomfortable, or it's a little too chilly, you can easily retreat to your warm bed (and you can leave the older kids where they are!). Plus, the fridge is nearby for late-night snacks, and you don't have to deal with any unpleasant shared shower blocks. It's the perfect mix of adventure and convenience, offering your kids a fun camping experience with all the comforts of home.

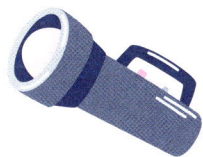

BUILD AN OBSTACLE COURSE

Building an obstacle course with your kids is a fantastic way to combine fun, physical activity and learning – all in one energetic session! Whether indoors or outside in the garden or the park, creating a course will help develop your child's motor skills, coordination and even problem-solving abilities. Plus, it's a great opportunity to teach them about teamwork as they work together to complete the challenges.

For younger toddlers, stay low to the ground! Set up cushions to jump over, tunnels made from cardboard boxes to crawl through and a "balancing beam" using a strip of duct tape or a scarf on the floor. Activities like hopping on one foot, crawling under chairs or rolling a ball through obstacles will keep them moving and engaged. Not only will they have a ball, but they'll also improve their gross motor skills.

For older kids, you can make the course a bit more ~~dangerous~~ interesting. Add more complexity with rope to limbo under (or jump over), a few water hazards (hello, garden hose) or perhaps a balancing challenge where they have to carry something on their head without dropping it. You can also time them to add a competitive edge, turning the obstacle course into a race between siblings. No need for real danger, but a "floor is lava" section (using pillows or mats) never hurt anyone!

If it's a rainy day or you don't have a garden, there's plenty of indoor fun to be had. Transform your living room into an adventure zone by using sofa cushions, blankets and chairs – and tie some string to various items of furniture to create a "laser" section to climb over and under. You could even add a small bell to the string so it sounds when the "laser" goes off.

By creating these playful courses, you're not just ensuring a fun afternoon – you're also building your children's confidence, boosting creativity and sneaking in some important skill-building along the way.

MAGNET FISHING

If you're looking for a new and fun activity to do with your kids, have a go at magnet fishing. Forget gruesome bait, sharp hooks and squirming fish – magnet fishing lets you search for hidden treasures without any of the grim stuff. Armed with a seriously strong magnet and some rope, your kids can pull up all sorts of treasure from rivers, ponds or canals – like old coins, tools and forgotten metal objects. Make sure to keep a close eye on what they find in case it's something sharp. Anything that you don't want should be disposed of safely.

Magnet fishing is entertaining for all ages – toddlers will love the excitement of pulling up little trophies (just make sure to watch them near the water) and older kids can get competitive about who finds the coolest stuff. Magnets aren't expensive and can be reused over and over again, making them a great long-term investment and activity for family days out. And who knows, you may end up finding some real treasure!

PICNICS

Picnics are a timeless activity, but they're also a fantastic way to make day trips more affordable. Whether you're heading into town or to the beach, packing a rucksack with lunch and a ball means you can enjoy the day without spending a fortune. For a city trip, why not hit the free museums, then head to a park for your picnic and a game of football? Your biggest expense? An ice cream!

Beach days are perfect for picnics. Children can spend hours upon hours hunting for shells, building sandcastles and paddling in the waves – and you'll have the packed lunch ready for when hunger strikes. Bringing your own food not only saves money but also keeps your picky eaters happy – no need to hunt down a restaurant that serves sandwiches with the crusts cut off. Plus, it allows you to stay immersed in the day's activities without interruptions. It's a fun, budget-friendly way to make the most of any day trip.

MOTHERS ARE LIKE GLUE. EVEN WHEN YOU CAN'T SEE THEM, THEY'RE STILL HOLDING THE FAMILY TOGETHER.

Susan Gale

SWEET NOTES

Leaving little notes for your children in their lunchboxes, coat pockets or on their pillows is an effortless and eloquent way of showing them how much you care, even when you're not physically with them. These sweet, thoughtful gestures can brighten their day, remind them they're loved and contribute to a sense of security.

For a child, finding a note from a parent can make them feel connected, valued and emotionally supported, especially during moments when they might feel nervous or unsure, such as when they're having a tough time at school. It deepens the bond between you and reinforces the idea that you're always there for them, even when you're apart.

Whether it's a funny joke, a reminder of how proud you are or just a simple "I love you", these notes can offer comfort and reassurance, creating positive memories for all of you – it may even become a tradition that they eventually pass on to their own children.

KITCHEN CHAOS

Cooking doesn't have to be one of those chores you just have to get through before the bedtime routine, and by cooking together as a family, you can make it much more fun than the regular daily grind. It's a great way to teach your kids valuable life skills, boost their confidence and bond over that chaotic kitchen energy.

For little chefs (ages 2–4), tasks like washing vegetables, stirring cake batter or tearing up lettuce for a salad are perfect. Okay, so they'll probably taste-test things they shouldn't (like flour), but it's all part of the process and you'll get some amusing photos out of it!

Kids aged 5–7 can start helping with more advanced tasks. Let them measure out ingredients or practise mixing and kneading dough. They can also help decorate biscuits, make sandwiches and crack eggs (make sure you have extra on hand, just in case).

For 8–12-year-olds, you can introduce them to actual cooking – supervised, of course. They can start learning some basic knife skills, chop vegetables (stick to soft ones until they're competent) and even help with cooking on the hob (just keep an eye on them and be ready with a spatula rescue or a fire extinguisher!). This age group loves the feeling of responsibility, even if it means your kitchen has to become a temporary disaster zone.

Older teens can tackle more complex tasks and learn to cook easy meals by themselves – pasta dishes, simple stews or baking a cake. By now, they're also capable of cleaning up… theoretically. Make sure you check the recipe and ingredients before they start so you don't walk in halfway through and find them trying to blowtorch a crème brûlée!

In the end, cooking as a family not only teaches valuable skills but also builds confidence, encourages teamwork and creates memories – just remember to delegate the washing-up.

FAMILY BUCKET LIST

Creating a family bucket list is a fun, exciting way to dream big together while planning awesome adventures. It's like writing down all the crazy, exciting and maybe even slightly impractical things you've always wanted to do – only this time, you're dragging the kids along. Suggestions don't have to be expensive and can be completely goal orientated for the future – like running a marathon together or spending a whole week in your pyjamas, if you'd prefer. Bucket lists are a great way to teach kids about goal setting, prioritizing what matters most and teamwork.

Even if you don't cross off everything, just working through the list creates memories and brings everyone together. You can change and adapt the list as your kids grow older and watch in horror as "learn to climb a rock wall" turns into "family bungee jump" – but at least you'll have some hilarious stories to share!

REDECORATING?

Turn redecorating into a fun family project by creating a themed bedroom with your kids. Make sure you guide their choices so the design will age well with them. Try a forest theme with full-length woodland wall stickers, a green rug and artificial vines and fairy lights hung from the ceiling with small light clips. Or go "under the sea" and paint the walls blue, attach a fishing net to the ceiling with light clips and add sea creature or tropical fish stickers. If you have a limited budget, check out social media marketplaces for items that fit in with your theme.

Your kids will be thrilled to help bring the room to life – from choosing the décor and helping you paint to putting the finishing touches together. They can also assist with organizing storage solutions or picking out fun lighting options. The result will be a fun, imaginative space and they'll always remember the special experience of designing it with you.

Making memories with your family is less about planning the perfect day and more about being present for the magic in everyday moments.

OLD PHOTOS?

Tired of spending a fortune on wall-hung photos as your kids grow, only to throw them away a year later as they need updating? Those old canvases often end up gathering dust in the loft, never seeing the light of day again. Instead of letting them go to waste, why not repurpose them? Paint the canvases white (using some of that left-over ceiling paint hiding in the garage) and let your kids unleash their creativity by turning them into masterpieces using ready-mixed poster paint. Blank canvases are quite expensive, so this saves money and keeps your little ones entertained for hours. They'll be thrilled when their artwork is proudly displayed on the walls, plus you can update the canvases each year by simply painting over them again, preserving the memory by taking a photo first. A fun, budget-friendly way to refresh your home with personal touches while giving kids a creative outlet.

ENTREPRENEURIAL KIDS

If you feel like you're always repeating the same old activities with your children, consider something a bit different and try creating a small business together. Not only is it a fun way to spend time with your kids, but it also teaches them valuable life skills like financial management, work ethic, creativity and responsibility. Plus, kids love the sense of accomplishment that comes from building something from scratch – especially when they're making their own money!

You can start with something simple, like making fresh lemonade, friendship bracelets or keyrings to sell from a makeshift stall outside your house. Younger children can contribute by helping with the creative aspects – choosing colours, designs and assisting in the crafting process. Older kids can take on more complex tasks like managing orders or even handling the social media presence for the business.

Whatever business you decide to start, make sure you fully research the regulations around the product, and the rules around work for minors and tax implications, to ensure your business is legally complicit.

Once your children have mastered their new business methods, they'll likely come up with new and improved ideas. Motivated by the possibility of earning money, they might even choose to dedicate time to their business independently – leaving you with more time to focus on your own tasks or put your feet up. Mutually beneficial results!

"YES DAY"

Giving your kids a "Yes Day" (basically, you say "yes" to all of their requests) is a great way to let them experience a sense of control and freedom, within reason of course! While you're not going to let your six-year-old drive the car or your eight-year-old parachute out of a plane, you can guide them toward fun and safe choices. Suggest things the day before, like having ice cream for breakfast, building a blanket fort using all the sofa cushions or having a water balloon fight in the garden. Give them a limit on the amount of requests they can make so it doesn't get out of control! The memories they make during this rare day of freedom will stick with them, and they'll likely feel valued and more cooperative on other days – which can really come in handy when you're battling the school run!

IF YOU CAN DANCE
AND BE FREE AND
NOT EMBARRASSED,
YOU CAN RULE
THE WORLD.

Amy Poehler

Farewell

"Time and tide wait for no ~~man~~ mum."

Fourteenth-century English poet Geoffrey Chaucer once wrote, "Time and tide wait for no man." Today, this quote is more relevant than ever, except to be truly up to date, we need to change "man" to "mum"!

Time is an entity rarely afforded to mums who are constantly running around after everyone else and neglecting their own needs. But time isn't going to stop. It's not going to wait until your children are older and come back to find you. You can't store it up. And you can't get it back. So, you need to make the most of it, now.

Utilizing methods to save yourself time and ensuring that you keep yourself as a high priority can allow you to balance the daily grind with your own personal needs. The tips and strategies in this book have hopefully sparked ideas to help you reclaim your time and focus on yourself, because you deserve it! Whether it's organizing your home, mastering the art of meal prep or finding smarter ways to tackle house chores, these time-saving techniques are all about freeing up precious minutes to use on the things that matter most to *you* and your children.

Being a mum doesn't mean you have to lose yourself in the daily madness. Yes, you wear many hats – taxi-driver, chef, nurse, referee (to name a few) – but that doesn't mean your identity is limited to those roles. By finding ways to claw back time, you can focus on activities that bring you joy and help you recharge. Whether that's reading a book, taking a solo walk or simply having a quiet moment to yourself, these acts of self-care are essential to your well-being.

Remember, when you take care of yourself, you're better equipped to take care of everyone else and you have more energy and time to do meaningful things with your children. So as life's tides continue to roll, embrace the small changes that will give you more time, balance and fulfilment. This is your life too, Mama, and it's up to you to carve out the time to live it more on your own terms.

Calm Cards for Mums

978-1-83799-026-9

Card deck

A mum deserves to find calm every day and this gorgeous box of illustrated cards is the perfect way to help her unwind

Throughout motherhood, finding time for self-care is a challenge and all too often sacrificed for the day's to-do list and the needs of others. But all it takes is as little as five minutes - and the gentle advice on these cards - to instil peace. From learning the basics of deep breathing to small reminders that you are enough, these calm cards are the perfect antidote to times of strife, stress and everything in between.

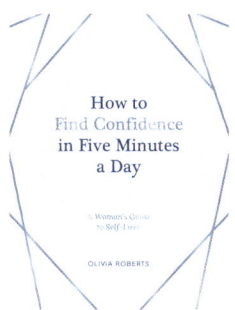

How to Find Confidence in Five Minutes a Day

978-1-83799-375-8

Hardback

Grow your confidence and embrace self-love with this proactive guide to becoming a stronger, more empowered you

Low self-confidence affects us all from time to time, but studies have shown that women are even more likely to avoid self-promotion and less likely to champion themselves. If you're someone who struggles to be your own cheerleader, then look no further. This empowering little book will teach you all you need to know to become the most confident version of yourself.

Have you enjoyed this book? If so, find us on Facebook at **Summersdale Publishers**, on Twitter/X at **@Summersdale** and on Instagram and TikTok at **@summersdalebooks** and get in touch. We'd love to hear from you!

www.summersdale.com

Image Credits

pp.1, 6, 78, 81, 103, 108, 122, 144 © Olena Illustrations/Shutterstock.com; pp.15, 17, 18, 19, 21, 24, 27, 28, 29, 30, 32, 35, 37, 39, 40, 41, 43, 47, 53, 56, 59, 61, 64, 67, 69, 71, 73, 75, 82, 85, 88, 89, 91, 92, 98, 99, 101, 102, 104, 110, 111, 117, 120, 121, 123, 126, 127, 131, 133 © PawLoveArt/Shutterstock.com; p.49 © Kingwardobe/Shutterstock.com; p.114 © v.iraa/Shutterstock.com; p.137 © WinWin artlab/Shutterstock.com; p.138 © barrirret/Shutterstock.com